T0163715

NUGGETS *of* WISDOM
for LIFE'S JOURNEY

"Marvin's weekly *Spiritual Messages* are good for the soul and will aid any Christian in their walk. He blends the old wisdom of the Bible with contemporary attributes so the meaning becomes concise and crystal clear."

—Mr. Kim N. Kershaw
(South Orange, NJ)

"Getting *Spiritual* information in proper measure."

—Ed Huggins
(Irvington, NJ)

"When times are hard, Marvin's *Spiritual Boosters* are a pick me up. It's good to know you have great resources at your disposal."

—Marc Bausch, Assistant Principal
(Livingston, NJ)

"I find Brother Marvin's *Spiritual Boosters* refreshing and an encouraging way to reconnect with God's Word. He uses current issues that are common to us all and binds them to God's Word, the Bible."

—Larry Gutierrez
(North Bergen, NJ)

"Marvin's *Spiritual Booster* has been encouraging, uplifting and timely. God's word is precise and accurate in each of his weekly messages. We are extremely grateful for Marvin's consistent commitment to the cause of Christ."

—Vernon and Jade Jones
(Mecklenburg County, NC)

NUGGETS *of* WISDOM *for* LIFE'S JOURNEY

MARVIN E. JOHNSON

NASHVILLE

NEW YORK • LONDON • MELBOURNE • VANCOUVER

NUGGETS *of* WISDOM *for* LIFE'S JOURNEY

© 2019 MARVIN E. JOHNSON

Published in New York, New York, by Morgan James Publishing. Morgan James is a trademark of Morgan James, LLC. www.MorganJamesPublishing.com

The Morgan James Speakers Group can bring authors to your live event. For more information or to book an event visit The Morgan James Speakers Group at www.TheMorganJamesSpeakersGroup.com

All scripture quotations, unless otherwise indicated, are from the Holy Bible, New Revised Standard Version (NRSV). Copyright 1989 by Oxford University Press. Used by permission. All rights reserved. Scripture quotations marked NKJV are taken from the New King James Version, original African Heritage Edition. Copyright 2007 by Judson Press. Used by permission. All rights reserved. Scripture quotations marked KJV are taken from the King James Version of the Bible.

ISBN 978-1-64279-142-6 paperback
ISBN 978-1-64279-143-3 eBook
Library of Congress Control Number: 2018948389

Cover Design by:
Rachel Lopez
www.r2cdesign.com

MorganJames PUBLISHING
Builds

with...
Habitat for Humanity®
Peninsula and
Greater Williamsburg

In an effort to support local communities, raise awareness and funds, Morgan James Publishing donates a percentage of all book sales for the life of each book to Habitat for Humanity Peninsula and Greater Williamsburg.

Get inv.olved today! Visit
www.MorganJamesBuilds.com

Presented to:

_____

From:

_____

Date:

_____

Dedicated to Monica, my beautifully, spiritually, and wonderfully made miracle daughter whom God has given to me and my late wife and bride of forty-five years, Sandra.

To my loving and very supportive sister, Marlene.

To LueQuincie L. Lee, a precious loving woman of God.

Every one of you has been an inspiration to me.

Contents

Foreword

For nearly three decades, I have been privileged to call the author of *Nuggets of Wisdom for Life's Journey*, my friend. Marvin E. Johnson, author, teacher, Christian Counselor, encourager and much sought after speaker, has written another profound piece of literature that is certain to ignite the spiritual fire within each reader.

It is exciting to be a part of this wonderful work. Its message is authentic, as it represents the true character and nature of Marvin. I fondly recall the first time we met. Two days after moving to a new community, I answered an unexpected knock at my door. To my delight and surprise, three friendly faces greeted me warmly, and welcomed me to the neighborhood. That encounter connected our spirits to begin a rich and fulfilling journey, as spiritual friends and brothers in Christ.

It is of the utmost importance for readers of this rich treasure to know that Marvin E. Johnson's words of wisdom have been inspired by his experiences and a deep place within his spirit, rooted in a steadfast love for God. He is a man of integrity whose faith, strength and message, are grounded in the Word of God.

As I have come to my ending "About the Author" like unto the book of Proverbs Chapter 16:9; which proclaims, "A man's mind plans his way, but the Lord directs his steps and makes them sure."

God's continued blessing, Marvin. Your faith in work is truly Heaven bound.

Brothers in Christ!

— **Dr. Glenn B. Wilson Sr.**,
Pastor of Pilgrim Baptist Church
(Newark, NJ)

Preface

This book of messages came about because of my bereavement for my wife and bride, Sandra. She passed away in 2014 after the forty-fifth year of our wonderful marriage, which was blessed by God.

These messages were all inspired by the Holy Spirit, the third member of the Trinity, "God in action," speaking through me to a weekly audience of 120 to 130 persons nationwide. Every Saturday morning, these recipients receive these by text message.

Initially, the content was written about a brief subject corroborated by scriptural quotations from the Holy Bible or by Christian books. As the messages gained momentum about what was to be addressed for any given week, they blossomed into a series. All of my messages include Bible verses.

Each topic is presented in seven parts, except for Part Two: Understanding Faith, which has six. The reader should note that seven is a symbolic representation of completeness.

The primary purpose of this book is to spread the good news (of the gospel) of Jesus Christ to a wider audience. Its secondary purpose is to challenge the reader to look through a different lens in order to live with a positive outlook.

— **Marvin E. Johnson**

Acknowledgments

This book follows my first book, *Desire Under the Sun: U.S.A.*, published in 1964.

My first acknowledgment is to God Almighty through the Holy Spirit inspiring me to write and document each message with scriptural quotes and researched commentary.

To my daughter, Monica, who has been incredibly supportive and has used her "God-given" expertise to help me with my vision.

To my sister, Marlene E. Holmes, LueQuincie L. Lee and Rev. Dr. Mary White Williams, I owe much gratitude for critiquing and editing my initial manuscript. Additional thanks to Barbara Kois, who helped to finalize my manuscript prior to publication.

Special thanks to Dr. Glenn B. Wilson, Sr., my neighbor and friend, for sacrificing his time to review the manuscript and write the foreword to this book.

To the many persons who agreed to receive my weekly messages and respond with their "Amen" or "OK", thank you. Your comments about the weekly readings and editorial suggestions have propelled me to transform my messages into a book.

Much appreciation to Carl Peterman, Larry Gutierrez, and Terriann Moore-Abrams for their special weekly responses. Special thanks to Chad Peterman for his legal advice/suggestions and W. Terry Whalin for his belief in my manuscript.

Many thanks to Morgan James Publishing: David Hancock, Jim Howard, Bethany Marshall, Nickole Watkins, Margo Toulouse and the rest of the team for their imprint on my book. You all have been outstanding.

To those persons who said that my messages should be written in a book for the world to read, you've been an amazing uplift for me.

Last but not least, to the readers. May you find inspiration and encouragement for your own life's journey through this book.

Part One

Understanding
Life's Journey

1

God's Love

This is the first in a series, written during the Lenten season, called "Understanding Life's Journey." We will have a better understanding of our life's journey if we first understand and appreciate what God did and said to us many centuries ago. In John 3:16 in the Holy Bible, New Testament, a re-read of this Scripture in the King James Version says it all. It also allows us to have a different perspective this time around and a good starting point.

"For God so loved the world, that he gave his only begotten Son that whosoever believeth in him should not perish, but have everlasting life." These are powerful words that give each of us hope for starting our daily walk and understanding life's journey."

Is Jesus Christ with you on your journey? Amen?

2

International Space Station

I n the last message, the focal point was on the great love God has for us. In this message, I want you to travel with me in your mind's eye and also by going to Google or another search engine where you'll now travel "400 km (or 249 miles) in low Earth orbit to the International Space Station (ISS); circling the globe every 90 minutes at a speed of about 17,500 miles per hour (28,000 kph)."[1] At the same time, the earth moves about our sun in a very nearly circular orbit. It covers this route at a speed of nearly thirty kilometers per second, or 67,000 miles per hour.

Stay on board with the well-trained, disciplined astronauts, and marvel at the view and your ride. Imagine the wonder of it all! Genesis 1:1 reads, "In the beginning when God created the heavens and the earth" and Psalm 24:1 tells us, "The earth is the Lord's and all that is in it, the world, and those who live in it."

The Holy Bible says it all, and it's where we can read about what God has created. We are also able to see the beauty of it all and call on the Holy Spirit who will live in us when we believe in Jesus Christ.

Seeing and feeling are believing and amazing! Amen?

1   https://www.wired.com/2015/09/whats-special-low-earth-orbit/
     Accessed September 25, 2017.

3

Resurrection and Ascension

M ark 16:5–6 reads, "As they (Mary Magdalene and Mary, the mother of James) entered the tomb, they saw a young man dressed in a white robe sitting on the right side; and they were alarmed. But he said to them, 'Do not be alarmed; you are looking for Jesus of Nazareth, who was crucified. He has been raised; he is not here.'"

To better understand our life's journey, we must *first* fully understand what took place a little over 2,000 years ago. Jesus Christ had already been crucified and was in His grave. But when we celebrate Easter/Resurrection Sunday, we remember that He arose from the grave and walked among the people of that time for forty days before His ascension.

Because of His ascension, we today have the presence of the Holy Spirit. We also have a hope for life eternal beyond the years we are permitted to live in this life. When Jesus Christ died for our sins, He and only He allowed each of us to have salvation, *if* we make the choice in our lives to claim Him as our Lord and Savior.

Now life's journey can be better understood! Amen?

4
Wisdom

In Proverbs 4:10–11 it is written, "The fear of the Lord is the beginning of wisdom, and the knowledge of the Holy One is insight. For by me your days will be multiplied, and years will be added to your life."

Take a long look at yourself in a mirror and search deeply to determine where you are on a scale of one to ten for wisdom in your life's journey; ten being the highest in wisdom. Be honest and modest, not boastful about yourself. After all, this is about you.

Wisdom makes common sense look good! Amen?

5
Self-control

In the previous chapter I spoke to you about wisdom. It is not listed as one of the personality traits to enhance your Christian life. But it is a key to all of those traits (fruit of the Spirit in Galatians 5:22) that will enhance your Christian life.

Your daily walk must have these traits within your personality to have the best walk on your life's journey. Proverbs 25:28 speaks about self-control. "He that hath no rule over his own spirit is like a city that is broken down, and without walls."

We must learn how not to act on our impulses by thought, word, or deed even when the temptation to do so is very strong. This is where the power of the Holy Spirit will lift you out of harm's way to walk away or to back off. However, you must first claim to personally know Jesus Christ.

Remember, consequences are not always seen at first! Amen?

6

Discipline

In the previous chapter I spoke about self-control. A direct link to self-control is discipline. Luke 4:8 tells us, "Jesus answered and said unto him, 'Get thee behind me, Satan: for it is written, Thou shalt worship the Lord thy God, and him only shalt thou serve'" (KJV). These words were being spoken by Jesus when He was in the wilderness for forty days and forty nights being tempted by Satan. This is an excellent testimony about where God has created within each of us an ability to state, "Get thee behind me, Satan," and he must flee because of your faith and consistent belief in Jesus Christ.

Although discipline can become a part of your personality, it must be developed by each of us over a period of time *if* we are to have it. Unfortunately, this is not realized by all persons.

Discipline, a powerful weapon! Amen?

7
God's Best for Us

T his is the last message in the section on Understanding Life's Journey. In the six previous messages I have introduced you to the various insights, views, and guideposts for understanding your journey through a different lens. Now I give you the "wrap" or conclusion for this very important section.

Much more could be written about our life's journey. However, while this section is inspirational, it is just another perspective for this moment in time for your life. A review is now in order to give you better footing for continuing along your way.

First, you were told how God loves you. Next, you traveled to the International Space Station (ISS). After that, you envisioned Christ's resurrection and ascension. Then you addressed wisdom, seized self-control, and practiced discipline.

Today, you can stand still for a moment to digest this section on Understanding Life's Journey. In Luke 12:7 it is written, "But even the hairs of your head are all counted. Do not be afraid; you are of more value than many sparrows." We must remember that God wants the very best for each of us. After all, He created us in His image.

We are somebody! Amen?

Part Two

Understanding Faith

8

Starting Your Faith

This section on Understanding Faith speaks to a very important area of your life that gives "glue" to the belief in our Lord and Savior Jesus Christ.

Our subject for today is found in Hebrews 11:1: "Now faith is the substance of things hoped for, the evidence of things not seen" (KJV). Here we are today, believing in our Lord and Savior Jesus Christ, whom we have not personally seen in the flesh or on the morning or evening news. We, however, believe because of the Holy Spirit, who speaks to our hearts and minds about Him and who lives in each one of us who has embraced Romans 10:9–10. Look that one up (see Chapter 34).

A very powerful testimony for starting your faith! Amen?

9

A Strong Bond

The previous message gave you the definition of faith. Now this message provides the hard part for many who are hearing about faith, but who are not sure how to take faith into their belief system.

Hebrews 11:6 is very clear about why we must embrace faith. "And without faith it is impossible to please God, for whoever would approach him must believe that he exists and that he rewards those who seek him."

What a strong bond between you and God! Amen?

10
A True Test

In James 2:26, we see that faith must be coupled with our works. It reads, "For just as the body without the spirit is dead, so faith without works is also dead."

We are now obligated, as followers of our Lord and Savior Jesus Christ, to show others by the way we walk and talk that Jesus Christ lives in us. This is a very serious task and a high responsibility. It is saying that we are believers in Jesus Christ. The true test is when others see us and we do not know they are looking at us. Does Jesus shine in us when and where they see us?

Now comes your true test in living! Amen?

11

A Booster Shot

Oftentimes when we think about a booster shot, we are about to go into another flu season. The booster shots are not for everyone. But they are highly recommended by physicians, other medical professionals, and pharmacists for different age groups to build up one's immunity against flu strains that attack mankind every year, and many times with very sick and sometimes fatal consequences.

A spiritual booster shot is from your request to the Holy Spirit living in you reinforcing your belief in God and His Son Jesus Christ, our Lord and Savior. This spiritual injection into your thinking has no restrictions for seasons of the year or hours of any given day. It is available daily, 24/7, with a timely spiritual message that you may hear on the radio, see on TV, or read in literature or on your cellphone, laptop, or desktop computer. You can also pray to God individually or with others for a prayer request.

First Peter 1:21 tells us, "Through Him you have come to trust in God, who raised Him from the dead and give Him glory, so that your faith and hope are set on God."

A booster shot for your faith! Amen?

12

Your Daily Challenge

I n Second Corinthians 5:7 we read, "For we walk by faith, not by sight."

Before you were born, God had already typed a very special spirit into your DNA that would allow you to explore different pathways on your life's journey. Fact check this by looking up Genesis 2:7. You are uniquely made, one of a kind, even if you are an identical or fraternal twin, triplet, etc. No one else is you and will never be. Absolutely nothing can duplicate the spirit that God and only God has breathed into you.

God also allows each of us as we grow and mature to freely make choices. When we accept Jesus Christ as our Lord and Savior, we not only have salvation, but we also glorify God. And God's angels are applauding your leap of faith.

Walking by faith, your daily challenge! Amen?

13
Your Glue

This is the last message in the section called Understanding Faith. In Second Timothy 4:7, we read that "I have fought the good fight, I have finished the race, I have kept the faith." This is one of the most powerful testimonies that you can state in your life *before* it is time for you to stop breathing. You do not want to be like one of those Titanic passengers going down with the ship, not having declared that you have accepted Jesus Christ as your Lord and Savior.

Remember, faith is the "glue" to your belief in Jesus Christ! Amen? I pray that this important and informative section on Understanding Faith has been inspiring and uplifting for you.

Part Three

God's Rules and Penalties

14

Ten Commandments

Y ou have often heard, "What goes around comes around." Well, if you live long enough, you realize that our God, who created the universe, has "rules and penalties" indelibly marked for us.

If someone has done "wrong" to someone, you sometimes witness that wrong coming back to bite that individual. A natural kind of payback or reaping what you sow, if you will. You may not see it, but it does come back somewhere in that person's life.

God wrote His laws (rules) known as the Ten Commandments, and He gave them to Moses on Mount Sinai many centuries ago. These very important laws are the foundation for all of our laws today and are found in Exodus 20:3–17 and Deuteronomy 5:6–21, where God stated, "Thou shalt and thou shalt not . . ." He also stated very clearly through His teaching to the prophets and the apostles over time, what our consequences (penalties) are when we disobey His Word.

These rules and penalties were confirmed with the birth and ministry of Jesus Christ.

Today, we have no excuses! Amen?

15

Reaping What You Sow

Traps or obstacles are along life's road to snare you, and when you yield to them you pay the penalty (consequence). What is our penalty when we yield to what God stated we should not do? The apostle Paul said in Galatians 6:7, "Do not be deceived. God is not mocked, for you reap whatever you sow."

If we repent and are truly sorry for our misdeeds, God is in the forgiving business. We must always keep in mind that God does not bargain with us. He already clearly stated His words and *He* created *us*, not the reverse. We should never put Him to the test.

When we repent of our sins, God always forgives us. Amen?

16
Works of the Flesh

Many people challenge the authenticity of the Word of God as written in the Holy Bible. They are called atheists, gnostics, believers of other faiths, and even Christians. But they do this at their own risk. The choice belongs to every person. No exceptions. God gives you the choice, so when you freely accept Jesus Christ as your Lord and Savior, this glorifies God.

In Galatians 5:19–21, the apostle Paul said, "Now the work of the flesh are obvious: fornication, impurity, licentiousness, idolatry, sorcery, enmities, strife, jealously, anger, quarrels, dissensions, factions, envy, drunkenness, carousing, and things like these. I am warning you, as I warned you before: those who do such things will not inherit the kingdom of God."

That warning is the penalty! It is a bitter pill. Believe it or not!

God's Word speaks to your heart and conscience! Amen?

17
Tangled Web

A debate continues about the authorship of "What a tangled web we weave when we practice to deceive." Was it Sir Walter Scott, William Shakespeare, or Edgar Allan Poe who first stated these words? Perhaps the content should override the "who" in this case.

God's rules give a more definitive description of people weaving their own web of deceit or just plain lying and doubling down. God's rules as written in the Holy Bible are to the point in Psalm 26:4–5: "I do not sit with the worthless nor do I consort with hypocrites. I hate the company of evildoers and will not sit with the wicked."

Once again, the Scripture describes the penalty in Proverbs 11:21: "Be assured, the wicked will not go unpunished." Powerfully stated!

A tangled web of deceit yields a long-term consequence! Amen?

18
Steps Marked

There are times when you may have no choice about whose space you may be in, such as family, friends, neighbors, people at work, events, or just plain waiting rooms.

Today's message is about the right place, wrong time. The place is where you thought you should be, but the timing may not be right. This is often heard in reference to catastrophic events locally and in our world today.

If you are a believer in our Lord and Savior Jesus Christ, you should thank God every day for His protection and for the Holy Spirit whispering into your ear and speaking to your heart to grant you safe passage through each day. God helps you to safely go from place to place on any given day. There are no guarantees, but you pray and you hope. Proverbs 20:24, tells us, "All our steps are ordered by the Lord, how then can we understand our own way."

Steps marked and penalties avoided! Amen?

19
Awakening Moment

When we look at our lives today, we may question, "Why is there such an imbalance between those who have and those who have not?" You may say, "I have confessed with my tongue that I love the Lord and believe in my heart that He lives in me today through the Holy Spirit." However, I am struggling and those who seemingly have it all don't believe or have any faith.

"So unfair!" you say. Who said, "Life has to be fair"?

One of life's keys, when found, is priceless, but it does not guarantee an instant change.

It is a fresh start. That key is knowledge. Proverbs 1:7 is clear: "The fear of the Lord is the beginning of knowledge; fools despise wisdom and instruction." Understanding this helps you become acquainted with God's rules and penalties for living.

Life's awakening moments! Amen?

20
Penalties Avoided

Today's message introduces a new acronym, FSD: Faith, Self-control, Discipline, to give you the mental and spiritual strength for obeying God's rules—a martial arts defense for your thinking.

FSD is an inspired mindset filter, coupled with your scriptural whole armor of God (see Ephesians 6:10–17) that equips you with God's finest protection against Satan and his cohorts (visible and invisible). This filter, and the whole armor of God planted deeply within your personality, will aid you when your temptations and hardships are great. It is a deadbolt lock of prevention.

Penalties avoided! Amen?

Part Four

God's View
of You

21

Remarkable View of You

W hen you were a child, did you ever wonder who you were, beyond what you saw in the mirror or were told? Well, guess what? I believe God's view of you was seen before you were conceived in your mother's womb. He has kept an eye on you from your very beginning. He knows you better than your doctors do. God also knows you better than your parents did or do know you.

We read in Psalm 139:13, "For it was you who formed my inward parts; you knit me together in my mother's womb."

A divine, blessed, and remarkable view of you! Amen?

22
Fantastic Creation

In the last message, I spoke about a divine, blessed, and remarkable view of you. It doesn't stop there! Psalm 139 continues our story in verses 14–16: "I praise you, for I am fearfully and wonderfully made, wonderful are your works; that I know very well. My frame was not hidden from you, when I was being made in secret, intricately woven in the depth of the earth. Your eyes beheld my unformed substance. In your book were written all the days that were formed for me, when none of them existed."

Can you imagine the incredible thought process behind God's love for you? That He made you the way you are? DNA that is uniquely yours. One of a kind! Even if you were an identical twin, triplet, etc., no one else is you. Even if you could be cloned, you would not be duplicated in spirit. That is why God speaks to us personally through our hearts, and as believers our hearts are sealed by Jesus' blood to Him when we accept Jesus Christ as our Lord and Savior.

Each of us is a fantastic creation! Amen?

23
Tragic Choices

Today's message is a spiritual perspective that goes to the heart of why we see mankind with a personality of "the good, the bad and the ugly." The marked moment in history was written many centuries ago, before Christ (BC). The date is unknown. The Bible states clearly that the event was the tragic day when Cain killed his brother Abel and tried to cover it up. Life was never the same after that, right to this day.

Genesis 4:8–9 tells us, "Cain said to his brother Abel, 'Let us go out to the field.' And when they were in the field, Cain rose up against his brother Abel, and killed him. Then the Lord said to Cain, 'Where is your brother Abel?' He said, 'I do not know; am I my brother's keeper?'"

Under what we call "normal circumstances," God has given choices to us. We can commit to a lifestyle of good and honorable behavior or bad and quite frankly ugly actions. It truly saddens God when He sees us as having taken life's road that is totally contrary to what He wants for us. This life is temporary. Eternity will be forever in heaven or in hell.

Tragic choices and bad excuses! Make yours better. Amen?

24
Prayer

Whether you are employed, retired, or unemployed, this message is for you. You have now showered or bathed, shaved (some men), groomed yourself, shined your shoes, applied makeup (women), done your hair, polished your nails, dressed, and taken a final look in the mirror and a last-minute check of what to take before exiting the house, apartment, condo, or hotel room.

Breakfast at home or on the run is part of your daily routine, if you eat breakfast. Whew! What a daily rush before getting into the car or truck, walking or running for the bus or train or waiting for your morning ride. Was there any time for exercise or prayer and meditation? With all of this, God was watching you. Did you take time to communicate or take a moment for Him as you started your day?

In Colossians 4:2–4 we read, "Devote yourselves to prayer, keeping alert in it with thanksgiving. At the same time pray for us as well that God will open to us a door for the word, that we may declare the mystery of Christ for which I am in prison, so that I may reveal it clearly, as I should."

Prayer is your most powerful communication link to God! Amen?

25
Hope

Today's message addresses the seeds of faith and hope planted within each of us when we were created. These same seeds were allowed to blossom as we grew older in each of us according to God's divine schedule. Remember, faith is the glue for your belief in Jesus Christ. As a believer, the Holy Spirit dwells within you.

On August 5, 2010, thirty-three men were trapped 2,300 feet below the surface of the earth for sixty-nine days at the San Jose mine in Chile. Chilean media put the miners' chances for survival at "less than 2 percent."

Each miner, deep down in his heart, believed and hoped that he would be saved; and each was saved. This story greatly magnifies the fact that God's view of you allows you to reach out to Him and conquer what appears to be impossible. This can be applicable to you for crisis situations or relationships in your life when you never thought you would come out of your "tunnel" or see daylight again.

Second Thessalonians 2:16–17 talks about hope from God: "Now may our Lord Jesus Christ himself and God our Father, who loved us and through grace gave us eternal comfort and good hope, comfort your hearts and strengthen them in every good work and word."

Hope beyond the impossible! Amen?

26
Powerful Forces

Today's message is about angels. Have you ever encountered an angel somewhere along your life's journey? You have if you experienced a close call with death and you are now reading this message. The memory of that or those incident(s) is very vivid in your mind, never to be forgotten. You did not survive by happenstance. You survived because God and only God did not want you leaving this life yet.

God's view of you is constant, and He makes sure that you are not out of His sight no matter where you are, 24/7. Psalm 91:11–12, Matthew 4:6, and Luke 4:10–11 talk about angels. "For He will command his angels concerning you to guard you in all your ways. On their hands they will bear you up, so that you will not dash your foot against a stone."

God's powerful forces are guarding you! Amen?

27
More Wisdom

A ARP (American Association of Retired Persons) allows you to claim that you are a senior citizen at age fifty. But God's view of you provides a whole different perspective. Unfortunately, God calls many home before they ever see the "big 5 - 0." But our daily prayers should reflect that we are given a more global view for living when we are older, as in "been there and done that."

Wisdom for some, but regretfully, maybe not for all. We must never forget that we can be educated and unschooled. We can also be schooled and uneducated. And there is nothing worse than an educated fool. Do you know someone like that? He or she may benefit from your wisdom if you can talk to them or better yet pray for them if you cannot reach out to them.

Psalm 71:17–19 says, "O God, from my youth you have taught me, and I still proclaim your wondrous deeds. So even to old age and gray hairs. O God, do not forsake me, until I proclaim your might to all generations to come. Your power and your righteousness, O God, reach the high heavens."

More wisdom granted when older! Amen?

Part Five

God's Incredible Math

28

God's Math Unmatched

When you hear about math or arithmetic, you often think about something related to school or homework. Well, allow this message to give you a whole new perspective on math and calculations from God's point of view. When God created this world, He placed planet earth on "an axial tilt of about 23.4 degrees" (see Wikipedia on axial tilt) and spun it around so it would make one complete rotation in twenty-four hours around the sun. Also, a point near the equator of the earth must move at close to 1,000 miles (1,600 kilometers) per hour. The calculations as we know them today, *all*, not some, emanated from God in the very beginning of time and have been shared with individuals through the ages.

God made sure that future generations would have a way back to Him (God the Father) when Jesus (God the Son) walked the earth and the Holy Spirit was given to believers when Jesus ascended back to heaven. Jesus' death on the cross demonstrated God's love beyond anything the human race could have imagined.

Matthew 19:30 is evidence of God's most meticulous math when Jesus spoke to His disciples, "And even the hairs of your head are all counted."

God's math unmatched! Amen?

29
God's Hidden Figures

There is no doubt about the fact that down through the ages, we have seen and witnessed incredible displays of genius in men, women, and children who had extraordinary math skills. This was recently shown in a movie called *Hidden Figures*, an untold true story about three brilliant Negro women (as they were called at the time) who were gifted by God with a mathematical knowledge that made the late astronaut John Glenn's first orbital trip into space around the earth and return a success.

These black women mathematicians were Mary Jackson (played by Janelle Monáe), Katherine Johnson (played by Taraji P. Henson), and Dorothy Vaughan (played by Octavia Spencer). They were "known as the computers in skirts who worked on the Redstone, Mercury and Apollo space programmes for NASA"[2] in the early 1960s.

John 3:34 gives testimony to this, "He whom God has sent speaks the words of God, for he gives the Spirit without measure."

God's hidden figures! Amen?

---

2   https://www.theguardian.com/film/2016/dec/11/black-women-mathematicians-nasa-john-glenn-space-race.

30
Seen by God

I n this message, I am privileged to take you a little deeper into God's reasons for the mathematics given to mankind. Think about it. How could you build or construct anything or calculate distances or keep track of time or do much more without mathematics? It would be impossible!

God gave all the other sciences a basic foundation through math. He saw and knew all other sciences before and beyond mathematics. Today we have a tendency to take our measurements for granted.

In Job 38:1, 4–5, a testimony is written, "Then the Lord answered Job out of the whirlwind: Where were you when I laid the foundation of the earth? Tell me if you have an understanding. Who determined its measurement surely you know! Or who stretched the line upon it?"

Seen by God before creation! Amen?

31
Math on Calendars

God's Incredible Math gave us the marking of the days, weeks, months, and years in a sequential measurement of time. This has also allowed mankind to mark the years in time and split time as we know it today: before Christ (BC) and Anno Domini (AD) "in the year of (our) Lord."

Numbers 1:1 gives testimony to God keeping track of time: "The Lord spoke to Moses in the wilderness of Sinai, in the tent of meeting, on the first day of the second month, in the second year after they had come out of the land of Egypt."

God's incredible math on calendars! Amen?

32

Math in a Census

Every ten years, the United States government does a population count of our citizens and other required data. Let us stop for a moment to think about what God is also doing daily. After all, it was He who created mankind on the sixth day of a magnificent creation. He has a tally of all who have come into the world and gone, not to mention all persons still living, by name, not yet named, gender, and age. What a massive undertaking, but nothing too great for God to handle.

God's Incredible Math continuously marks time, not only from day one, but right to the moment God's Son, Jesus, came to the earth. God continued His marvelous revelation when Jesus declared to His disciples that He must depart so that the Holy Spirit could come to them. What a plan, one that was totally off all human charts for comprehension.

Numbers 1:2 says, "Take a census of the whole congregation of Israelites, in their clans by ancestral houses, according to the number of names every male individually."

God's incredible math can be seen in a census! Amen?

33

God's Reservation

Of course, God doesn't just throw all of His census information into a void. He stores all that He has done down through the centuries in a very meticulous recording in the heavenly realm. Those who are to be with Him are written in the Book of Life. This is one of the reasons you have been given a name at birth. Your name has been saved forever, beyond the grave, as well as for recognition and responses from God while walking in this life.

God's Incredible Math is reserved for you. Praise God for your identity being recorded for eternity. Revelation 20:12 tells us, "And I saw the dead, great and small, standing before the throne, and books were opened. Also another book was opened, the book of life."

God's reservation for you! Amen?

34

Unmatched for You

This is the last message in the section God's Incredible Math. There is no need for you to know your number. This is the one time in your life that you do not need a number for a reservation. All you need to know is that you have confessed with your lips that you have accepted Jesus Christ as your Lord and Savior and believe in your heart that God has raised Him from the dead. That is your ticket for the reservation of salvation that God has for you. This is so simple and easy that it literally defies imagination.

Unfortunately, many people *do not* accept this one-of-a-kind step along life's journey. This is one of God's Incredible Math concepts in action for you.

We read in Romans 10:9–10, "because if you confess with your lips that Jesus Christ is Lord and believe in your heart that God raised him from the dead, you will be saved. For one believes with the heart and so is justified, and one confesses with the mouth and so is saved."

God's incredible math—unmatched for you! Amen?

Part Six

The Holy Spirit's Mission

35

Alive and Real

To understand the Holy Spirit's mission, you must first understand in your heart who He is and believe with your mind that He exists. Jesus Christ, God the Son, told His disciples after His crucifixion and resurrection and before His ascension that He must leave and that the Holy Spirit was going to come into the world. This is indeed one of life's baffling mysteries, but it's true!

Jesus clearly states in John 14:16–17, "And I will ask the Father, and he will give you another Advocate, to be with you forever. This is the Spirit of truth, whom the world cannot receive, because it neither sees him nor knows him. You know him, because he abides with you, and he will be in you."

The Holy Spirit is alive and real! Amen?

36
The Holy Trinity

Not only is the Holy Spirit alive and real, He is also part of the Trinity, God in three persons. He is omnipresent, omnipotent, and omniscient. These three characteristics explain the big why and how God is able to touch every person born into this life as we know it. Yes! This is astonishing, baffling, and one of life's great mysteries. All we have to do is believe in Jesus Christ as our Lord and Savior. No one else! When that occurs, the Holy Spirit will indwell, or live in you.

Romans 5:5 tells us, "And hope does not disappoint us, because God's love has been poured into our hearts through the Holy Spirit that has been given to us."

God the Father, Son, and Holy Spirit! Amen?

37

Salvation

One day, on a date unknown to mankind, God will fulfill what Jesus promised when He walked the earth. The Holy Spirit's mission today is to gather all of us (His flock) who are under His wings and who have claimed Jesus Christ as Lord and Savior. Jesus Christ is the only way when the rapture comes. One must always remember that it will come suddenly, worldwide, and without warning. Mankind has been told by Jesus of these things when He walked on this earth and we have now been informed by what has been written in the Holy Bible.

In John 14:3 we read, "And if I go and prepare a place for you, I will come again and will take you to myself, so that where I am, there you may be also."

Salvation, what a blessing! Amen?

38
Through Christ

M any times we hear about the word *salvation*, but we don't go beyond its meaning until we feel a need to go to church or are listening to someone talking about it in another setting. Traditionally, for Christians (Protestants and Catholics), this occurs on Sundays when we listen to a sermon or a spoken word about God.

Salvation is preached, and you must feel a need within you to accept its meaning and purpose in your life. This is where and when the Holy Spirit makes His presence known to you. This can happen anywhere and at any time. There are no restrictions or limits on what the Holy Spirit's mission is for you.

First Thessalonians 5:9–11 says, "For God has destined us not for wrath but for obtaining salvation through our Lord Jesus Christ, who died for us so that whether we are awake or asleep we may live with him. Therefore encourage one another and build up each other as indeed you are doing."

Salvation through Jesus Christ! Amen?

39

A Must Acceptance

This message addresses a subject that many of us do not want to talk about. That subject is what will happen to you when you die. Interestingly, some persons don't seem to care. They live day to day and take very high risks in living; and many pack "heat" to prove their point. They are not officers of the law. There have been many books written about what comes to our minds about this unavoidable event that claims every person, male and female, rich and poor. There are no exceptions to this inevitable moment for all of us.

Thanks be to God, who created us, that we have an Advocate, the Holy Spirit, who wants us to believe in Jesus as our Lord and Savior.

We read in John 14:25–26, "I have said these things to you while I am still with you. But the Advocate, the Holy Spirit, whom the Father will send in my name, will teach you everything, and remind you of all that I have said to you."

Will you accept this offer without delay? Amen?

40

You Are a Witness

One must always remember, if you ever have to say, "What if," it is too late! Tomorrow is never promised to you. This is the purpose of these inspired messages, to share God's Word and have a spiritual interaction with you. They are also written for you to share with loved ones and others with whom you may speak. They are another tool for you that may make it easier for the Holy Spirit to come into someone else's life through you.

It is truly amazing how the Holy Spirit speaks. Acts 1:8 tells us, "But you will be my witnesses in Jerusalem, in all Judea and Samaria, and to the ends of the earth."

You are also a witness! Amen?

41

Tongues Should Shout

T oday, when we are on the scene of an accident and not involved in it, we may become a reluctant witness, not really willing to testify to the authorities on what we saw. Well, guess what? We are witnesses to an event that took place a little more than 2,000 years ago by our belief in Jesus Christ. It is remarkable and also true that "if you confess with your lips that Jesus is Lord and believe in your heart that God raised him from the dead, you will be saved" (Rom. 10:9). The Holy Spirit's mission to mankind has made this so. Now we must share what we are a witness to with others.

In Luke 12:8, Jesus gives a very strong comment first to His disciples before addressing the thousands who had gathered to hear Him speak. "And I tell you, everyone who acknowledges me before others, the Son of Man also will acknowledge before the angels of God."

Our tongues should shout "Jesus!" Amen?

Part Seven

Jesus, a Challenge to Others

42

Choose Wisely

This section addresses a very serious subject that causes us all at some time to ask, "Why are there so many other religions beyond the Christian belief?" If you think about it, when you were born, did you have anything to say about who your parents were? No. The chances are if your parents or guardians were of a particular faith or religion, you too became acquainted with that same belief.

If, however, you were born into a Christian or even a Jewish family, you had a head start on being introduced to Jesus Christ. If that was not your circumstance, you were faced with many other religions, or no religious belief, that challenged your thinking and belief system. The choice is very clear without any doubt, when you look at and examine all religions. The Christian faith that introduces you to Jesus Christ shines in a special way.

Acts 4:12 says, "There is salvation in no one else, for there is no other name under heaven given among mortals by which we must be saved."

Jesus Christ or not? Choose wisely! Amen?

43
Much Older, My Choice

Perhaps when you were a youngster, your parent(s) or guardian(s) stated to you, "There are two subjects you do not discuss with persons in your presence unless you want to get into an argument or even a fight." They were religion and politics.

Naturally, as you grew older, you may not have heeded that advice. You were now a student with knowledge to enable you to defend your position and belief, and you were schooled in various topics.

But we all must make a choice. The Bible tells us in Joshua 24:15, "But as for me and my household, we will serve the Lord."

Now that we're older, it's our choice! Amen?

44

A Celebration of Christmas

C hristmas is a season of the year that is celebrated worldwide with much joy and anticipation. December 25, as you know, is when Christians and others celebrate the birth of Jesus Christ. It is also a date on which many people choose not to acknowledge it. That is their choice. Yes, God has given mankind the ability to make choices of our own free will based on our own beliefs.

If you embrace Christmas as a time to celebrate the birth of our Savior, this glorifies God.

Isaiah 7:14 tells us, "Therefore the Lord himself will give you a sign. Look, the young woman is with child and shall bear a son, and shall name him Immanuel."

Choose to celebrate Christmas! Amen?

45

A Celebration
Now and for Glory

When we celebrate Christmas, it brings great joy to be shared with gift giving, family and friends gatherings, and most importantly, worshiping the birth of our Lord and Savior Jesus Christ. The flipside to all of the above is an absence of any presence of Jesus Christ in many households. When we think about this sharp contrast, the reality stares each of us in the face. Not all persons believe in what you believe in.

Again, the Holy Bible explains the Holy Spirit's part in Christmas. We read in Matthew 1:18, "Now the birth of Jesus the Messiah took place in this way. When his mother Mary had been engaged to Joseph, but before they lived together, she was found to be with child from the Holy Spirit."

A celebration now and for glory! Amen?

46
The Only Way

Your Christmas celebration may give you a little down time from your daily routine, providing you with a chance to increase your personal library of knowledge. It's truly amazing how knowledge gives you an insatiable thirst for more information on any given subject.

This is true when you sift through information about the various religions of the world. Yes, Jesus Christ *is* a challenge to others because unlike any other, *He is alive* and is able to live in you when you claim Him as your Lord and Savior. Psalm 86:8 states, "There is none like you among the gods, O Lord, nor are there any works like yours."

Jesus Christ is the only way! Amen?

47

Wow, That's It!

Now we must embrace Jesus Christ to experience the fullness of living our lives in the best way possible. But we also now know that forces seen and unseen will be seeking to disrupt our very best efforts for our life's journey. Who said this would be easy? God knew us from the beginning of time, and we will never be alone.

God has allowed us to have a strong connection to Him. This is through the Holy Spirit who walks with each of us every day when we have accepted Jesus Christ as our Lord and Savior. No matter how much or how long you may search, believe it or not, there is no other way.

We see in Romans 6:22–23, "But now that you have been freed from sin and enslaved to God, the advantage you get is sanctification. The end is eternal life. For the wages of sin is death, but the free gift of God is eternal life in Christ Jesus our Lord."

Wow, that's it! Amen?

48

A Course Change

Now that you know Jesus, you should share with others your walk with the Holy Spirit living in you. This does not mean "a holier than thou" attitude when you are around other people. Quite the contrary. It means we should reflect the positive characteristics the Holy Spirit displays in us, including a personality that definitely excludes any negatives you once shared with others.

Philippians 2:3–5 tells us, "Do nothing from selfish ambition or conceit, but in humility regard others as better than ourselves. Let each of you look not to your own interests, but to the interests of others. Let that same mind be in you that was in Christ Jesus."

These words give clear evidence of the positive personality change we can have when we know Jesus.

Hallelujah, you're on a course change! Amen?

About the Author

Marvin E. Johnson is a retiree, prayer warrior, family genealogist, and published author of his first nonfiction and now rare book, *Desire Under The Sun: U.S.A.* (1964), a book that gave "observations on the state of society in America, particularly as it regards to civil rights . . . " in the 1960s.

He is a graduate of Fairleigh Dickinson University with a BA degree in Psychology and of The Stonier Graduate School of Banking at Rutgers University with a Diploma of Graduation in Banking.

Nuggets of Wisdom for Life's Journey is his second published book.

Morgan James
Speakers Group

www.TheMorganJamesSpeakersGroup.com

We connect Morgan James published
authors with live and online events
and audiences who will benefit
from their expertise.